SONATA No. 19

GOTTFRIED REICHE
(1667-1734)

Moderato (in two) **11**

Reiche, the first trumpeter of J.S. Bach, introduced the fugal form for tower music.
In this sonata we have a wonderful fugue followed by a recitative-like Adagio and a
moving Grave. The sustained trumpet melody of the Grave is echoed in the tuba.

MMO CD 3905
MMO Cass. 6003

FOUR PIECES

JOHANN PEZEL
(1639-1694)

Moderato

Intrade

The suite, a popular instrumental form during the baroque era, was a group of related pieces in highly stylized dance rhythms. An Intrada usually introduces the suite and in this vigorous one, every part has a thematic entry which should be "hammered" out.

3 beats precede music.

$\textstyle\frac{1}{2} = 42$

Andante

Sarabande

The Sarabande started life as a wild and primitive dance of the American Indian. However, one hundred years after it reached Europe, via the Spanish conquerors, it had become a stately court dance. In this stirring Sarabande, the Bb major scale of the tuba holds the work together. Homophonic (chordal) pieces such as this one call for careful blending with no one of the parts "sticking out."

MMO CD 3905
MMO Cass. 6003

4 beats precede music. ♩=112

Bal

The two sections of this "ballet-like" piece are played slightly faster when repeated. This, in the style of the time, adds some variation to the performace. Watch the last two measures, they crescendo (grow louder) but the antiphonal bell tones between the upper voices should not be hidden.

Gigue

Allegro (in one) D

trpt.

E

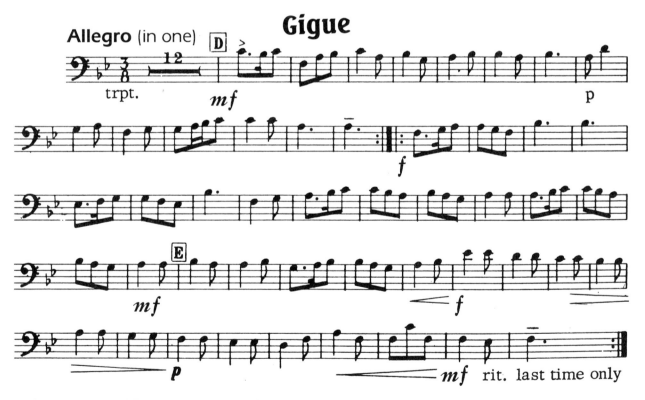

The Gigue was traditionally used to bring a suite to a close. Notice how Pezel uses the first subject, only turned up-side down (inverted), for the second section. Once again the thematic entries are hammered out by all the players who then immediately recede into the background.

Canzona per sonare No. 1
La Spiritata

GIOVANNI GABRIELI
(1557-1612)

This famous "chain" type canzona has three contrasting sections in style as well as meter.
Hold each note for its full value and play smoothly with a minimum of accents.

TWO PIECES

Honie-Suckle

ANTHONY HOLBORNE
(-1602)

2 beats precede music. ♩=100

Allegro maestoso (in two)

Night Watch

2 beats precede music. ♩=108

Allegro

Here is an example of modal harmony full of surprises for our major and minor ears.

SONATA No. 2

Hora Decima (Leipzig. 1670)

JOHANN PEZEL
(1639-1694)

4 beats precede music. ♩=120

Moderato

The first two sections of this sonata are full of echoes, an important feature of baroque music. The last section begins with a chordal cadence, again echoed followed by a very graceful polyphonic section.

6

SONATA *from* DIE Bänkelsängerlieder

Anonymous
(c. 1684)

4 beats precede music. ♩=112

Allegro

rit.

Adagio

This ingenious piece gives the effect of two choirs echoing one another. The trombone plays first with the trumpets, then with the horn and tuba, adjusting its attack accordingly.

Canzona per sonare No. 2

GIOVANNI GABRIELI
(1557-1612)

There is a return to the opening section in this exciting piece at letter D so help us keep the middle section alive by accenting your three repeated eighth notes starting with letter B.

MMO CD 3905
MMO Cass. 6003

SONATA No. 1

This engaging sonata begins with the trumpet singing a minor mode melody over an ostinato bass. The bass line, a descending chromatic scale, was a favorite of baroque composers. The second section, a fugue, is another familiar baroque form. Examine your part for thematic entries (the theme starts in the tuba) and play these <u>out</u>, and everything else except the ending, <u>under</u>.

5 beats precede music. ♩ = 42

JOHANN GEORG CHRISTIAN STÖRL
(1675-1719)

2 beats precede music. 𝅗𝅥 = 60

SONATA No. 22
from
Hora Decima (Leipzig, 1670)

JOHANN PEZEL
(1639-1694)

The trumpets are pitted against the lower voices throughout this typical tower sonata.
Play with your partner or partners in mind, matching their articulations and dynamics.

MMO CD 3905
MMO Cass. 6003

THREE DANCES

from

Het derde musyck boexken (Antwerp, 1551)

TILMAN SUSATO
(1500-c. 1560)

2 beats precede music. ♩ = 72

Moderato **Ronde**

2 beats precede music. ♩. = 50

Allegro (in one) **Salterelle**

The Ronde and Salterelle found here are charming examples of a single melody adapted to two contrasting dance rhythms.

MMO CD 3905
MMO Cass. 6003

11

3 beats precede music. ♩ = 56

Pavane *(Si par souffrir)*

Andante

Here is a good test for your breath control.

MMO CD 3905
MMO Cass. 6003

12

Music Minus One TENOR SAX Compact Discs

__ MMO CD 4201 Easy Tenor Sax Solos, Student Editions, 1-3 years
__ MMO CD 4202 Easy Tenor Sax Solos, Student Editions, 1-3 years
__ MMO CD 4203 Easy Jazz Duets with Rhythm Section, Beginning Level
__ MMO CD 4204 For Saxes Only, Arr. by Bob Wilber

Music Minus One TROMBONE Compact Discs

__ MMO CD 3901 Easy Solos, Student Editions, Beginning Level vol. 1
__ MMO CD 3902 Easy Solos, Student Editions, Beginning Level vol. 2
__ MMO CD 3903 Easy Jazz Duets, Student Editions, 1-3 years
__ MMO CD 3904 Baroque Brass & Beyond
__ MMO CD 3905 Music For Brass Ensemble

Choice selections for the Trombone, drawn from the very best solo literature for the instrument. The pieces are performed by the foremost virtuosi of our time, artists affiliated with the New York Philharmonic, Boston, Chicago, Cleveland and Philadelphia Orchestras. The Julliard School, Curtis Institute of Music, Indiana University, University of Toronto and Metropolitan Opera Orchestra.

Beginning	Intermediate	Advanced	Level
__ MMO CD 3911	Per Brevig, Metropolitan Opera Orch.		B
__ MMO CD 3912	Jay Friedman, Chicago Symphony		B
__ MMO CD 3913	Keith Brown, Soloist, Prof. Indiana Univ.		I
__ MMO CD 3914	Jay Friedman, Chicago Symphony		I
__ MMO CD 3915	Keith Brown, Soloist, Prof. Indiana Univ.		A
__ MMO CD 3916	Per Brevig, Metropolitan Opera Orch.		A
__ MMO CD 3917	Keith Brown, Soloist, Prof. Indiana Univ.		A
__ MMO CD 3918	Jay Friedman, Chicago Symphony		A
__ MMO CD 3919	Per Brevig, Metropolitan Opera Orch.		A

The repertoire and editions used in the Laureate Series correspond to the approved music lists of various Music Education Associations and may be performed as contest solos in State Music Festivals. Contest regulations, such as time limitations have been taken into consideration.

Music Minus One TRUMPET Compact Discs

__ MMO CD 3801 3 Trumpet Concerti Haydn/Telemann/Vivaldi
__ MMO CD 3802 Easy Solos, Student Edition, Beginning Level vol. 1
__ MMO CD 3803 Easy Solos, Student Edition, Beginning Level vol. 2
__ MMO CD 3804 Easy Jazz Duets with Rhythm Section, Beginning Level
__ MMO CD 3805 Music for Brass Ensemble
__ MMO CD 3806 First Chair Trumpet Solos
__ MMO CD 3807 The Art Of The Solo Trumpet
__ MMO CD 3808 Baroque Brass And Beyond
__ MMO CD 3809 The Arban Duets

Choice selections for the Trumpet, drawn from the very best solo literature for the instrument. The pieces are performed by the foremost virtuosi of our time, artists affiliated with the New York Philharmonic, Boston, Chicago, Cleveland and Philadelphia Orchestras. The Julliard School, Curtis Institute of Music, Indiana University, University of Toronto and Metropolitan Opera Orchestra.

Beginning	Intermediate	Advanced	Level
__ MMO CD 3811	Gerard Schwartz, N.Y. Philharmonic		B
__ MMO CD 3812	Armando Ghitalla, Boston Symphony		B
__ MMO CD 3813	Robert Nagel, Soloist, NY Brass Ensemble		I
__ MMO CD 3814	Gerard Schwartz, N.Y. Philharmonic		I
__ MMO CD 3815	Robert Nagel, Soloist NY Brass Ensemble		A
__ MMO CD 3816	Armando Ghitalla, Boston Symphony		I
__ MMO CD 3817	Gerard Schwartz, N.Y. Philharmonic		I
__ MMO CD 3818	Robert Nagel, Soloist, NY Brass Ensemble		A
__ MMO CD 3819	Armando Ghitalla, Boston Symphony		A
__ MMO CD 3820	Raymond Crisara, Concert Soloist		B
__ MMO CD 3821	Raymond Crisara, Concert Soloist		B
__ MMO CD 3822	Raymond Crisara, Concert Soloist		I

The repertoire and editions used in the Laureate Series correspond to the approved music lists of various Music Education Associations and may be performed as contest solos in State Music Festivals. Contest regulations, such as time limitations have been taken into consideration.

Music Minus One OBOE Compact Discs

__ MMO CD 3400 Albinoni Three Oboe Concerti Opus No. 3, No. 6, Opus 9 No. 2
__ MMO CD 3401 3 Oboe Concerti: Handel, Telemann, Vivaldi
__ MMO CD 3402 Mozart/Stamitz Oveo Quartets in F major (K.370; Op. 8 #3

Music Minus One DRUMMER Compact Discs

__ MMO CD 5001 MODERN JAZZ DRUMMING, 2 CD Set
__ MMO CD 5002 FOR DRUMMERS ONLY!
__ MMO CD 5003 WIPE-OUT!
__ MMO CD 5004 SIT IT!
_* MMO CD 5005 DRUM STAR
_* MMO CD 5006 DRUMPADSTICKSKIN
_* MMO CD 5007 LIGHT MY FIRE
_* MMO CD 5008 FIRE AND RAIN
_* MMO CD 5009 CLASSICAL PERCUSSION, 2 CD Set
* Winter '95/Spring '96 Release

Music Minus One BANJO Compact Discs

__ MMO CD 4401 Bluegrass Banjo
__ MMO CD 4402 Play The Five String Banjo, vol. 1, Dick Weissman
__ MMO CD 4403 Five String Banjo, vol. 2, Dick Weissman

Music Minus One BASS VIOLIN Compact Discs

__ MMO CD 4301 Beginning & Intermediate Bass Solos
__ MMO CD 4302 Intermediate & Advanced Bass Solos

Music Minus One INSTRUMENT METHODS

__ MMO CD 7001 Rutgers University Music Dictation Series
                6 CD Set   Deluxe Album $98.00
__ MMO CD 7002 The Music Teacher
__ MMO CD 7003 The Complete Guitar Method
__ MMO CD 7004 Evolution Of The Blues
__ MMO CD 7005 Art Of Improvisation, vol. 1
__ MMO CD 7006 Art Of Improvisation, vol. 2

MMO MUSIC GROUP, INC., 50 Executive Boulevard, Elmsford, N.Y. 10523-1325

MUSIC FOR BRASS ENSEMBLE

3905
TROMBONE